ALL THIS IS IMPLIED

Will Harris

HAPPENSTANCE

ACKNOWLEDGMENTS:

Thanks are due to the editors of The Rialto, The
Oxonian Review and The Poetry Review, in which
some of these poems (or earlier versions) first
appeared. Thanks also to The Complete Works,
and to Sarah and Richard. These poems are for my
parents and Aisha, with love and gratitude.

'Allegory' uses words and phrases from William
Langland's Piers Plowman, as well as from
George Herbert and Robert Hayden.

Printed by The Dolphin Press
www.dolphinpress.co.uk

First published in 2017 by HappenStance Press,
21 Hatton Green, Glenrothes, Fife KY7 4SD
nell@happenstancepress.com
www.happenstancepress.com

CONTENTS

Mr. Harris, after a reproachful glance, squatted down upon his hams. [...] For a little he was vexed by opposite currents in his blood, then they blended, and he belonged to no one but himself.

— E. M. Forster

OBJECT

X → Y What have you taken?
Y → X What you have taken.

X → Y What have I taken?
Y → X What you have taken from me.

X → Y I have taken nothing from you.
Y → X Then I have taken nothing.

MOTHER'S COUNTRY

(Jakarta, 2009)

The shutters open for landing,
I see the pandan-leafed
interior expanding
towards the edge of a relieved
horizon. Down along
the wet banks of the Ciliwung
are slums I have forgotten,
the river like a loosely
sutured wound. As we begin
our descent into the black
smog of an emerging
power, I make out the tin
shacks, the stalls selling juices,
the red-tiled colonial
barracks, the new mall ...
It is raining profusely.
After years of her urging
me to go, me holding back,
I have no more excuses.

HALO 2

There were those walls where brochure-like
paintings of a young Christ showed
his hairless body pricked with blood, aglow.
The artist, by a fine excess, had meant
to advertise his suffering. Late one night

playing Halo 2, I saw myself in what
I saw on screen and, from Beaver Creek
to Uplift, shot anything that moved:
the birds singing in the artificial trees;
the true self nothing more than the self as seen.

SELF-PORTRAIT IN FRONT OF A SMALL MIRROR

I pay close attention to the shape of my eyes, how my eyelids slope down towards the ridge of my nose—that fold of skin, which I will learn is the epicanthic fold, no more an indicator of race than my stubby little fingers or the mole at the centre of my chest. Just different. I am making a self-portrait in front of a small mirror propped up on my pencil case. How can I know that when I put aside the mirror, as I must, to encounter the world *with* and *through* those eyes, there will be questions: *where are you from? are you Korean? speak Chinese?* At seventeen, at Borders, I will say my books are for an English degree and the man behind the counter will grin, call me a bright boy, and though it may be nothing—as he says it, I see myself reflected in the glossy wall display behind him—I will feel accused. When I open my mouth in shops, though my voice shrinks into a weird RP, I will accept the illusion of the colonial elite, other in blood and colour but English in taste. The illusion will remain intact long after I am presumed foreign, after a stranger tells me to *fuck off back home*, after a barman—standing in front of a row of spirits, endlessly mirrored—asks for my ID, refuses to accept my name as my own. *Will Harris?* My nasal bridge which, being lower-rooted, draws a fold of skin over the corners of my eyes, marks me out—as it does these words—for special treatment. But I must, and will, put aside the mirror.

NAMING

Some uncouth name upon the native rock
  —William Wordsworth

I was myself stone,
at one with the elements,
at home—say it, *home.*

Words I gathered, sense
I framed in form; a whetstone
to hone thought against.

Seeing itself worked
on a different principle:
agent-less, unmarked.

Then one day a child
mistook me for his own bare
stone, and there inscribed

first his, then my, name.
For weeks afterwards I cried.
Still, I bear the shame.

BEE GLUE

'Break a vase,' says Derek Walcott, 'and the love
that reassembles the pieces will be stronger than
the love that took its symmetry for granted.'
When I read this I can only think *who broke it?*

In the British Museum, two black 'figures'
(they don't say slaves) beat olives from a tree;
a 'naked youth' stoops to gather the fallen
fruit. The freeborn men are elsewhere, safe

behind their porticos, arguing the world's
true form. They talk of *bee glue*, used
to seal the hive against attack, later called
propolis, meaning that it has to come
before—is crucial for—the building of a state.

Today it's summer and bees hum inside
the carcase of a split bin-bag. A figure passes,
is close to passed, when I see her face, half
shadow, glazed with sweat or tears, the folds

beneath each downcast eye the same
dark brown as—oceans off—my grandma, Mak.
I want a love that's unassimilated, sharp
as broken pots. That can't be taken; granted.

My dad would work among the blue and white
pieces of a Ming vase—his job to get it
passable. He'd gather every part and after days
assembling, filling in (putty, spit, glue),
draw forth—not sweetness—something new.

JUSTINE

In our matching blue uniforms,
I can't stop from staring as Justine
lifts up her skirt, removes her penis,
pees. At school the next day,

not knowing who to trust, our eyes
barely meet in the playground. Justine
won't talk or eat. Her dad has gone
abroad. At lunch I see her pour

a full salt-shaker in her water, drink
and retch, cry heavy adult tears.
I try to hold her but she weighs
too much. I'm so angry at Justine.

IDENTITY

With all this book learning, it's easy to lose
track of the body, but as I thumb through
A Cultural History of the Senses, I feel the full
weight of transcendence. Back when
Mum first came to London, she waitressed
at a Thai restaurant in Gants Hill. She says
the prawn toast would always slip off the plate
as she made to set it down, and one day
she spilt a whole plate on that guy who hosted
Restoration. Over three decades later
Chinese Indonesians are still keeping their heads
low (neither China nor Indonesia is home)
and here, as ever, the self must be embodied
or—like those oily sesame seeds on Griff Rhys Jones—
                                        embedded.

YELLOW

Think of Chung Ling Soo who,
a century ago, his smooth
face greased and pigtail
bobbing, brought the wonders
of the East to the London
Hippodrome. A blend
of grace and speed, his face
impassive as a clay
soldier's, he was an early
master of the linking rings
and wove a braid so fine,
they say, he made of it
a gift to the Empress Dowager.

Then think of Ching Ling Foo,
a conjurer from Peking
who one day browsing through
the news caught sight of Soo's
impassive face (his own
but strange) and went
to London—midwinter, mid-
depression, fog so thick
the rooftops looked like they
were under sea—to call
his double out. Drunk suitors
followed day and night
pulling at his hair. He did
two shows. No one came.

He grew impatient, wrote
bluntly to *The Times*
and turned a row of empty
seats into a flock of geese.
The next week, he was gone.

Now think of Soo and Foo
at the same time but
separately: a blue sky as
reflected in a clear blue lake,
water above and water
below. There's Soo
doubled-over on stage,
gun smoke clearing, real
blood running down his long
silk shirt. *Lower the curtain!*
A nasal brogue (his own
but strange) rings through
the theatre, fades.
                    Elsewhere,
in a corner of the Yellow
River Valley, Foo is sleeping
underneath a pinkish plum tree,
dreaming he's suspended
by his ankles in a sealed
water-tank, pigtail floating
up across his eyes. He tries
to pull the loose knot free

but only pulls it tight.
Bound and gagged he feels
the muscles slacken
from the back of his neck
down to his anus, his
calves, his anonymous
toes, around which billows
the yellow squit of his
final movement.

WITH CORNFLOWERS

A girl twists a stalk of rye
about her wrist like
a bracelet. She sees her father
at the plough and wants

to pick a cornflower, its dark
blue—almost purple—
colour threaded through
with grief, among the weeds.

She wants to go and pin
one to his chest. And all this
is implied, though
the photograph itself

shows just a field of rye
with cornflowers.

FROM 'THE ARK': I

Placement is all. The world revealed
by words/things, even nakedness,
is made by placement. Every field,
blurring boundaries, subject less
to its own vision than the total
arrangement of parts, is blind. Love,
having taken a view of the whole,
knows wholeness not enough.

The Tradescants, whose love of *strang*
things filled a whole house full
of diverse beasts and ornaments,
went beyond pleasure, seeking sense.
They made themselves an Ark and sang
relation, placing. Which is all.

CURED

A shrinking in the memory
From some forgotten harm.
   —Christina Rossetti

The start of a new term.
She pushed on me a tupperware
of rendang which I stowed
down the back of my cupboard.

Emotions likewise, out
of sight, were kept from harm;
my art, for art's sake, cured
and spiced. Once exposed

things rot, they date. But what
forgotten harms grow spores
unseen? I found it thick-furred
months later, like the art

I made, my self-regard.
Nothing is or can be closed.
We take our natural course,
are moulded, gasp for air.

FROM THE OTHER SIDE OF SHOOTER'S HILL

                              you saw an ambulance speed past
a row of stationary cars, though at a distance you couldn't hear
the siren and it looked to be moving slowly like a police car in a silent film
(driving slowly so as to appear at a normal speed in playback)
and you thought you saw the Keystone cops crowded into a single car
chugging along the road to your little niece's birthday party
where they would fall over themselves in a heap at her doorstep
and you started crying. And when you arrived at my flat you told me
about the ambulance and the Keystone cops and started crying
again—I did too—and I asked if everything was OK. Yes,
everything's OK, you said (suddenly embarrassed), but wait,
why am I telling you this? Don't you dare think about using me
in a poem, making me into some sad female cypher, my life
a series of symbolic events: the ambulance representing mortality,
my niece—I don't know—a hysterical desire for kids. Hey hey,
I said, what about the Keystone cops, how do they fit in?
If I say this in a poem, it isn't to defer responsibility but because
I reject the possibility of narrating any life other than my own
and need a voice capacious enough to be both me and not-me,
while always clearly being me. Fine, you said, pouring us
a cup of black tea. Once, I said (changing tack), I was given
a pellet gun for my birthday and without my knowing a friend
started aiming it at passers-by—or, he claimed, at pigeons—
until a neighbour called the police. In his defence he asked how
anyone could mistake the puck of a pellet gun for that of a real gun.
He sounds like a real jerk, you said. Starting to relax, to laugh,
you told me about a recent dream in which you were trapped
in a silent film, your every movement seen as slapstick, no one
able to hear you scream. Maybe we should watch some Percy Stow,
I said, and put on *How to Stop a Motor Car*, a minute-long silent film
featuring a car that slices a policeman in two before bouncing off

another man's butt. Hilarious, right? But it's Stow's 1908
version of *The Tempest* that's his masterpiece. He has Ariel,
freed from the bole of an oak tree, do a curtsey—she's just
a child—and scare off Caliban by turning into a monkey.
How great is that? But the cast, you said, who are they? A bunch
of Edwardian amateur actors and enthusiasts, I said. The girl
who plays Ariel might even have been the daughter of one.
She must be dead, you said. Obviously, I replied. But by this stage
in the evening I was tired, my lips moving slowly, and though
I could see you were in distress it was like the ambulance you saw
moving slowly, silently across the other side of Shooter's Hill.
I do want children, you said, but not yet, not in this world.
In playback, I knew, not only would we appear to be talking
comically fast, but it would be impossible to tell who was speaking.

FROM 'THE ARK': II

John Tradescant the younger, sole heir
to his father's good parts, resolved to make
a catalogue. He wanted Adam's peace
before the fall. Instead, before the year
was out he'd buried his small son and hidden

the draft, its shopping list of rarities
grown common. Among so many scarce
and far-flung things, he brooded on what can't
be kept, or what had led him to suppose
this rainy cosmos ours. The old mistake.

Inheritance is not passed down, but grows
within us, feeds off weakness, blares
importance. See the way it falls unbidden,
the oceans slowly filling, partial, slant.

SOMETHING

Instead of listening to you
I'm watching an advert in which
fresh cream is being whisked into
a froth and the inside of a passion fruit
scooped out, and it isn't right
morally that these images should
impinge on us when I want to be
listening to you, neither of us
having to ask what it is the other's
thinking, what it is that's not
being said.
             Please, let the something
unsaid between us be as pure and
forgiving as the flow of water
from a bathroom tap. Or, more
specifically, from the faucet
turned on by Robert Creeley
in the middle of the night
to hide the noise of his own
shy piss, trying not to disturb
even slightly the sleep
of the woman he loves.

ALLEGORY

Under a brood bank on a bourne side
I lean and look until the lapping water
sends me into a sleep so sound a vision
comes upon me without warning
and I wake up in a suite of seatless
rooms. A man who calls himself X
pulls me close—close enough to smell
the perfume on his collar—clasps
my palm and places in it a mirror that,
though appearing to reflect the world,
rings round it a contingent blur,
through which the thronging streets
look empty, unenclosed. In a haze
of hunger I can hardly move. X grins.
Behind him there is Y who eyes me up,
finicky as a feather-duster. Outside
the far-heavens loom, the streets tiny
as a toy-set. Y's fingers fuss about
X's face. *Be long-lived, loved by all,*
he says. Several stories high, sealed in,
the skyline sleek and lunar-white,
Y says: *Youth is a window, briefly open.*
If not flung wide your days will fester.
The room is airless, dry, the mirror's
edges marred with dust and sin—
my dust, my sin. X grunts assent.
I turn back, searching for the bank
on which I sat before. No one stops me
as I dive out of the door. Uprooted,
free to roam, I run across the road

and, heading south, past vacant shops
and parkland gone to seed, soon find
a house like mine, much as I left it. Same
shoe-rack, stock of spices, foreign
sweets, but in a low-lit corner of the living
room, there are pictures of me pinned
to a floor-strewn map. You (yes, *you*)
are waiting, watching. I try to talk
but, nothing like your bold breme self,
you speak a drone-like dreamer's
dialect, obsessing over shadows
on a screen. I'm blabber-mouthed,
my eyesight bleared. Your arms are
folded like my mother's, fraught face
filled with hurt. *Have you eaten?*
You look hungry. Light catches
on our old net curtains, throws
its spindly pattern on the ceiling:
a tall tree's splayed leaves spreading
as the light dims. Deep dark.
I look up through a latticework
of leafless branches, roof replaced
with empty space. The carpet turns
a slug-wet green, gives way. An elder
tree appears, its blistered bark
like my great-great-grandma's
bound and broken feet. *How long*
have I lain lone and dreaming?
I look up and she looks through me.
My aunts and uncles fumble before

taking flight, lose their bearings,
fall; their fall broken by leaf-moult,
they cry. An untaught, tongueless
cry. On a low twig hangs the hoarded
image of a man whose features match
my own, who, jailed for the sin
of race, remains among the unmet.
I hear his friends, relations, more unmet,
churn in their graves, the charnel
stench still fresh. No bourne to call
their own, their rotting bodies rootless.
X waits for no one. *No one*, he says.
On my feet, the lamplight bright,
smells of sage from the kitchen,
sounds of knives being sharpened.
Y sets the table. *Sit and eat*, says X.
Purge the past. Put it finally past care.
Hungry as I am, my stomach hard,
I can only brood on how I came here:
on the bankside and the mirror marred
with dust; on the lapping stream
I watched until the whole world
lagged and left me drifting down
into a dream, beyond which I cannot
see. *How long have I lain lone*
and dreaming? I smell the white
wine sauce, the sizzling flesh.
I feel my fist against the tabletop,
the wounds I cannot wash or wipe
away but know are real. They're

calling me to eat. I grope for naming
words that might make grief
comparable. I look to you there
slouched, unspeaking; the elder tree
outside. If I cannot speak to you,
at least I might speak at or with
or through you; in spite of absence,
so to spite it better. Do I sit with X?
Or set out on the forked path,
the losses growing, days scattered,
attachments incomplete? They're
calling me to eat.

IMAGINE A FOREST

Your voice foreign on the foreign trees,
you hear yourself as others hear you, hear
your voice as formed around a lack:

a falling stone seen from the stone's
perspective. Falling, falling, fall—